The Heart of Happiness
WORKBOOK

13 Techniques Using Mindfulness and Humor to Manage Stress and Find Happiness

Christy Eidson

CHRISTY EIDSON

Copyright © 2019 Christy Eidson

All rights reserved.

ISBN: 9781099136955

DEDICATION

Thank you to my daughter, Allison. I love you!

CONTENTS

	Acknowledgments	i
1	Introduction	1
2	Getting started on the path to happiness	4
3	How do I spend my time?	11
4	Negative self-talk and obstacles	23
5	What is the ANSWER to happiness?	29
6	SMART goal setting	40
7	Exercises	49
8	Find balance in my life	58
9	Re-evaluate my goals	65
10	Using the 13 techniques	74

ACKNOWLEDGMENTS

This book would not have been possible if not for my great grandparents, George and Elsie Eidson, who raised me. They are long gone, but their tough love prepared me for the real world, whether I was ready or not. We did not have a lot, but I knew that they loved me. I am also grateful for the love of my daughter, Allison.

I am so thankful for the support and encouragement of my friends Jana Mandes, Carolyn Pachuilo, Amy Delvin, Sissy Debut, Sandra Dee Nicholson, Ellen and Mark Greenbaum, and Maria Tucker who inspired, helped me proofread, and bounce ideas off.

I want to thank Vanderbilt University for keeping me alive! If it wasn't for the staff and surgeons, I would not be here to write this book.

And finally, I want to mention Randy Alexander, who is pictured in the book with his dog, Rufus. He always saw the best in people, and his life's mission was to spread happiness and cheer. (Also pictured are my dogs Roscoe and Freddie.)

1 INTRODUCTION

If you are reading this, more than likely you have read *The Heart of Happiness*. If you have, thank you! But that is just the beginning. This workbook is a companion to that book, and it helps you go on to the next level of your transformation.

There are many books on motivation, anxiety and depression, stress management, and personal transformation. Rarely, do any of them discuss happiness and how to achieve it. In this book, you will be able to define stress and identify stressors, discover helpful and effective stress management techniques that have been proven to work, and develop a plan to reach your goals. This book will also help you realize what happiness means to you. Similar books may cover one of these topics, but I wanted to create one book that encompasses all of them.

Stress is a normal part of everyday life, but not all stress is bad. Stress is the body's natural defense against danger. Stress can be a motivator to get you off your keister and turn thoughts into actions.

Sometimes we put things off until the time is just right. Or sometimes we delay because we don't want to do it unless we do it perfectly. Well, I've got news for you. There is no right time and there is no such thing as perfect! That is not to say that perfectionism cannot work in your favor, but it can only work if you put it into action. Any action is better than no action at all. Remember, the thousand-mile journey starts with one step. The hardest part is just showing up! Don't put it off until tomorrow, because tomorrow never comes. You only have today.
We may try to take steps to help us overcome our procrastination, but to no avail.

We may make deadlines for ourselves, but if they are not concrete, they will not work. Then, when we don't stick to them, we beat ourselves up when our goal is not reached or deadline not completed. This sinks us further in our hole of procrastination, because we feel defeated.

We become so transfixed on the outcome that it prevents us from even starting. We are looking at the process all wrong. It is not the destination that we should focus on, but the journey. We need to be involved in the total course of events. We need to be in the moment. After all, the end result is not what makes you happy, even though we believe that it will. It is the process that leads to happiness.

This book creates the foundation for your new path. When completing this book, it is important that you take your time, really think about your answers, and above all else, be very honest with yourself about your answers.

Now more than ever, we need to find and implement methods to deal with stress in our lives.

Here are some ways:
- Laughter - The Mayo Clinic writes that laughter can "stimulate circulation and aid muscle relaxation, both of which help reduce some of the physical symptoms of stress."
- Get a pet or watch cute animal videos. No, seriously! - One paper from *Frontiers in Psychology* reviewed sixty-nine studies and concluded that interacting with animals lowers fear and anxiety in people. Part of the reason for this lies in oxytocin, a hormone that, among its other jobs, reduces stress. Interaction with animals pumps more oxytocin to your brain.
- Smile - Smiling helps lower stress, lowers heart rates, and actually makes you feel better.
- Exercise - Even if you are tired, exercising gives you more energy. It lowers stress and increases endorphins.
- Unplug from technology – it is proven that constant communication increases stress.

- Meditation - reduces stress, improves concentration, increases acceptance, and improves cardiovascular and immune health.
- Yoga - can lessen chronic pain, lower blood pressure, reduce insomnia, and increase flexibility.
- Tai chi - strengthens muscles, increases flexibility and balance, and lowers blood pressure.
- Forest bathing - It is scientifically proven that Shinrin-yoki, or forest bathing, boosts the immune system, increases NK cells, and reduces blood pressure.
- Reiki - reduces stress, brings about inner peace and harmony, balances mind and emotions, relieves pain, and speeds recovery from surgery and illness.
- Aromatherapy - Relieves stress, has an antidepressant capacity, increases memory, boosts energy levels, speeds up healing and recovery, alleviates headaches and pain, enhances the immune system, and aids in sleep.

"The way to get started is to quit talking and begin doing." ~ Walt Disney

2 GETTING STARTED ON THE PATH TO HAPPINESS

I think that most of us can agree that happiness comes from feeling that all of our needs are being fulfilled. It can be described as a feeling of satisfaction and contentment. When people have a sense of well-being, it could be said that they have a sense of happiness. When most people are happy, they experience joy. These are positive emotions and experiences, but that does not mean that happy people don't experience negative emotions like sadness, anxiety, or anger. A happy person has better tools and coping mechanisms to deal with those negative emotions when they arise. They may have different ways of processing those emotions that others have not. They may even find meaning in those emotions. Happy people are still going to experience negative emotions, because they are human. They still experience stress, but it is how they handle those stresses that determine their happiness. Most often, instead of seeing stress as resistance, they will look at stress as an opportunity.

The Basics about Me

Overall, how happy do I feel right now?

On a scale of 1 – 10:

What does happiness mean to me?

_____

_____

_____

_____

What people, places, things, or activities make me happy?

_____

_____

_____

_____

What am I interested in and passionate about?

_____

_____

_____

_____

What are the things that I want to do "someday" or "when I have enough time"?

_____

_____

_____

_____

If money were not an issue, what would I want to do with my life?

_____
_____
_____
_____

What are my strengths?

_____
_____
_____
_____

What are my weaknesses?

_____
_____
_____
_____

When I reach my small goals, what will I do to reward myself?

_____
_____

_____

_____

What groups can I join, locally or online, that can help me network and motivate me toward my goals?

_____

_____

_____

_____

Who are some people that are doing what I want to do? How did they get to where they are?

_____

_____

_____

_____

What are my past successes?

_____

_____

_____

_____

What action can I do today to move me closer to my goals?

_____
_____
_____
_____

Does my environment support my goal? (Ex: if I want to quit smoking, is my environment smoke-free?) Can I change my environment? (Ex: make environment non-smoking)

_____
_____
_____
_____

When I visualize my finished goal, what does it look like? How do I feel? What does it sound, look, feel, and even taste?

_____
_____
_____
_____

What are my goals? Which ones are the most important? Prioritize them in order.

_____

_____

_____

_____

Do I feel like I have more energy first thing in the morning or in the evening? What is my "peak" time? What tasks can I work on during these times?

_____

_____

_____

_____

First, I must decide what it is that I want to do. Second, I must determine why. I have to ask myself: "Do I want to be ____ because ____ or ____?"
For example: "Do I want to be a <u>writer</u> because of <u>passion</u> or <u>money</u>?"

According to Dr. Joe Dispenza, there are five types of motivation:

- Purpose
- Personal connection
- Ethics
- Ego-centered
- Money

Money is your lower level motivation, whereas, purpose is the higher level. The reason why is very telling on how committed you are to reaching your goal. If it's just for money, how invested are you really? If it is because you are so passionate about it that you can't imagine doing anything else, you are going to be much more invested in accomplishing your goal. "I want to be an author with a self-published book on stress management, because I have an important message to put out into the world that can help a lot of people with the same issues that I have." That is a much stronger **WHY** than "I want to be an author to make a lot of money."

Why do I want to do this goal?:

_____

_____

_____

_____

_____

3 HOW DO I SPEND MY TIME?

Take some time to really look at your day-to-day schedule and see where your time is spent. Keep a log for a week and see if you can find where time could be better spent or what activities you may have to cut down on.

Day 1	Date:
Activities	**Time Spent Daily**
Sleeping	
Getting ready for the day *(shower, breakfast, getting dressed, etc.)*	
Working	
Commute	
Leisure *(TV, games, reading, etc,)*	
Eating	
Exercise	
Social	
Chores *(laundry, cleaning, etc.)*	
Shopping	
School, learning	
Other	

Day 2	Date:
Activities	**Time Spent Daily**
Sleeping	
Getting ready for the day *(shower, breakfast, getting dressed, etc.)*	
Working	
Commute	
Leisure *(TV, games, reading, etc,)*	
Eating	
Exercise	
Social	
Chores *(laundry, cleaning, etc.)*	
Shopping	
School, learning	
Other	

Day 3	Date:
Activities	**Time Spent Daily**
Sleeping	
Getting ready for the day *(shower, breakfast, getting dressed, etc.)*	
Working	
Commute	
Leisure *(TV, games, reading, etc,)*	
Eating	
Exercise	
Social	
Chores *(laundry, cleaning, etc.)*	
Shopping	
School, learning	
Other	

Day 4	Date:
Activities	**Time Spent Daily**
Sleeping	
Getting ready for the day *(shower, breakfast, getting dressed, etc.)*	
Working	
Commute	
Leisure *(TV, games, reading, etc,)*	
Eating	
Exercise	
Social	
Chores *(laundry, cleaning, etc.)*	
Shopping	
School, learning	
Other	

Day 5	Date:
Activities	**Time Spent Daily**
Sleeping	
Getting ready for the day *(shower, breakfast, getting dressed, etc.)*	
Working	
Commute	
Leisure *(TV, games, reading, etc,)*	
Eating	
Exercise	
Social	
Chores *(laundry, cleaning, etc.)*	
Shopping	
School, learning	
Other	

Day 6	Date:
Activities	**Time Spent Daily**
Sleeping	
Getting ready for the day *(shower, breakfast, getting dressed, etc.)*	
Working	
Commute	
Leisure *(TV, games, reading, etc,)*	
Eating	
Exercise	
Social	
Chores *(laundry, cleaning, etc.)*	
Shopping	
School, learning	
Other	

Day 7	Date:
Activities	**Time Spent Daily**
Sleeping	
Getting ready for the day *(shower, breakfast, getting dressed, etc.)*	
Working	
Commute	
Leisure *(TV, games, reading, etc,)*	
Eating	
Exercise	
Social	
Chores *(laundry, cleaning, etc.)*	
Shopping	
School, learning	
Other	

Procrastination

Procrastination plagues most of us at one time or another. We know what we need to do. Why can't we just do it? We make lists, plan schedules, read self-help books, and watch motivation videos, but nothing seems to work. We spend the time that we put aside to complete our tasks by watching TV or surfing the internet. We are stuck to our sofas like gum on the bottom of a shoe. We cannot manage the strength to just get out of bed! We come up with tons of distractions to avoid doing what we need and want to do. We make convenient excuses for delaying our action. We create our own speed bumps and roadblocks. Most of the time, it is all based on fear.

We may try to take steps to help us overcome our procrastination, but to no avail. We may make deadlines for ourselves, but if they are not concrete, they will not work. Then, when we don't stick to them, we beat ourselves up when our goal is not reached or deadline not completed. This sinks us further in our hole of procrastination, because we feel defeated.

Why Do We Fail?

Why don't we achieve our goals?

- Procrastination
- Distractions
- Overwhelmed
- Self-Defeating/Negative/Self-Sabotaging
- Hardest Part: Getting Up, Getting Out, Getting Started

What makes us fail? We make lists, schedules, etc., but they don't work. Hours fly by wasted doing anything other than working on our goals.

- On sofa
- In bed
- Internet surfing
- Reading

These distractions are excuses to delay.

What do we need to do to combat this?

- Small, obtainable goals – avoid overwhelm – daily goals
- Accountability
- Flip your thinking (Negative to Positive)
- Find out what you want to do (and why)

We often may get overwhelmed by how enormous the feat may seem. It is easier for us to do nothing than to attempt to climb this mountain. But if we make small, obtainable goals for ourselves, we will avoid being overwhelmed. Instead of looking at the top of the mountain and thinking you'll never make it, focus on taking the first step. As in the old saying, a thousand mile journey begins with one step. Before you know it, you will be fifteen steps into your journey, and then fifty, and so on. The trick is to not beat yourself up if you go a day with only making one step.

When you begin working out at the gym, it may seem like you have bitten off more than you can chew. Ten minutes on the treadmill may seem like a million years. But soon, you will build up to twenty, and before you know it, you are doing forty-five minutes. Once you get in the habit of hitting the gym, you miss it if you have to skip a session. It becomes part of your routine and part of you, but you had to work up to it to get to that point.

Eric Clapton did not wake up one day, pick up a guitar, and start playing. He practiced...a lot! In interviews, I have heard him speak of practicing for hours and hours every day. He practiced so much that his fingers would actually bleed. But he knew what he wanted. He knew that if he wanted to be the best in his field, it required strong determination and a great amount of work. But because of his dedication, he is the only three-time inductee into the Rock and Roll Hall of Fame.

You are going to fail sometimes. But that's okay. Those failures can also be looked at as steps to success. Every *"no"* that hear gets you that much close to a *"yes"*. A baseball player doesn't just pick up a bat and hit a home run. It takes practice. But even the best players face defeat. Reggie Jackson holds the record for most strikeouts with a career 2,597 strikeouts. That is a lot of failures. But he also has a record of 563 home runs. He struck out a lot, but it took those failures to create 563 successes.

Failure is not necessarily a bad thing. Our failures can be teaching tools. Thomas Edison once said something to the effect that "I didn't fail one thousand times. I've just found one thousand ways that didn't work." I was unable to find the actual quote, but you get the picture. It is not that we fall; it is that we get back up and do not quit. For example, if one were to drop a rubber ball, it doesn't just stay down; it bounces back. And the harder you drop it, the stronger it bounces back.

One reason that we fail to take action is due to our lack of focus. You may have given yourself a deadline, but it is not concrete. A passive deadline creates no sense of urgency. Then, if we do not stick to our deadlines, we beat ourselves up when our goal is not reached or deadline not completed. That only makes us feel terrible about ourselves and further makes us avoid taking future actions. We are our own worst enemies.

At times, we may beat ourselves up because we feel "stupid". It is totally fine to feel that way. It is arrogant to think that you know it all. You should constantly be learning. Be aware that you don't know it all. Be open to knowledge. It can also be said that you know more than you think you do. Give yourself some credit.

Timing is everything....WRONG! Again, there is no perfect time. We all think "I'll be happy when..." We have all been guilty of that from time to time. "I'll be happy when I get this position." "I'll be happy when I get a new house or a new car." You are putting your happiness on a time table. You are delaying your happiness for a time period that will never exist. Be happy now. You only have now. The past is gone, and the future never comes. You must be in the present. We are not guaranteed tomorrow. Anything could happen. We may face illness, loss, even death, so today should be lived to its fullest. And if you are living in the moment, it is senseless to deny yourself a second of happiness.

The hardest part about reaching your goal is starting. When working on *Annie Hall*, Woody Allen was interviewed and quoted as saying, "Eighty percent of success is showing up."

Why put off until tomorrow what you can do today! Procrastination is a major Achilles heel for most people. If your task falls under the important or urgent category, do it now. Once it is finished, you will feel so good about yourself and feel motivated to finish another task. Procrastination is only a way of putting off your success.

4 NEGATIVE SELF-TALK AND OBSTACLES

Two people are taking a cooking class, but they are both struggling. They both were having a difficult time making a soufflé. Both soufflés ended up burned and deflated. The first student beats himself up about it by saying, "I'm a failure. I can't do anything right. There is nothing that I'm good at." The second student thinks, "I've never been much of a cook, but this class is fun. Considering that I have never spent much time in a kitchen, I didn't do too terrible of a job, and I've learned a lot from my mistakes with this recipe." One exhibits a negative thought process, and the other displays a more positive one. Both of them had the same experiences and results, but their perspectives on them were different.

In the world that we live in, it is sometimes difficult to be positive. The news can be flooded with negativity. Even reading your social media feed can be a downer. But we have to remember that pessimism is not good for your health. Negative thinkers have higher rates of depression. Pessimists have higher levels of heart disease and do not live as long as more optimistic people. Optimists also experience greater productivity at work than their counterparts.

There are only two ways to look at things: Positively or Negatively. But we have to realize that the phrase "stay positive" is much more than just wishful thinking. It is a matter of rewiring our brains. We have been conditioned to accept and expect negativity, and it does not have to be that way. When we experience failures, instead of taking it personally, we need to look at them as learning experiences. Nothing is a mistake if we can learn something from it.

Negative Self-Talk

What negative beliefs am I holding on to that could be keeping me from my goals?

_____
_____
_____
_____
_____

How are my negative beliefs affecting me?

_____
_____
_____
_____
_____

What positive beliefs can I use to replace the negative ones? How will they more positively affect my life?

List 3 negative beliefs	Write down something that challenges each belief	Write a new positive belief to replace the negative one
Ex: "I'm afraid I'll fail."	"When I've worked hard, I've done okay."	"If I focus and work hard, I will likely do a good job."

Making Changes

What do I want to change right now?

_____

_____

_____

_____

What are the reasons that I want to make these changes?

_____

_____

_____

_____

_____

The steps that I plan to take in changing are:

_____

_____

_____

_____

_____

If I make this change, how will this make me feel?

___

What will it help me accomplish?

___

How will it affect my family and close relationships? How will it make them feel?

___

What can other people do to help me? (Ex: get a workout partner)

___

How will I know that my plan is working? (measure)

_____

_____

_____

_____

Welcoming and Overcoming Obstacles

What obstacles could interfere with my plan?

_____

_____

_____

_____

What can I do to overcome these obstacles?

_____

_____

_____

_____

5 WHAT IS THE ANSWER TO HAPPINESS?

In sales, the ANSWER might look something like this:

1) **Approach** the customer
2) Determine the customer's **Needs**
3) **Show** the merchandise
4) **Welcome** and overcome objections
5) **Encourage** the closing of the sale
6) Suggest **Related** items

Ask yourself these questions:

Who is your customer?

_____

_____

_____

What do these customers need?

_____

_____

_____

What can you do to fill this niche?

_____

_____

_____

What could their objections be?

_____

_____

_____

How can you persuade them to use your product or service?

_____

_____

_____

What else could you offer them to supplement what you are already offering them?

_____

_____

_____

But you can take a similar approach to setting and achieving your goals. The answer to happiness is ACTIONS.

Happiness has a direct correlation to motivation which leads to productivity. The Harvard Business Review conducted a study that found that people are more productive when they are positive. Thus, one can assume that having a positive outlook and being happy makes people more motivated.

ACTION Steps

Now, you go from talking to the talk to walking the walk. All the planning in the world does not matter until you put it into action.

Whether you want to achieve your goals or to make a sale, take these ACTIONS steps:

1) Approach your goal with **Action**
2) **Concentrate** on the goal/avoid distractions
3) Flip the Negative **Thinking**
4) Use your **Imagination**
5) Set small, **Obtainable** goals
6) Determine your **Needs** (for you and for your goals)
7) **Set** Intentions

Approach Your Goal With Action

All the planning in the world won't mean a thing if you don't put your plan into action.

Action:

- If you want to be a writer, sit in front of a keyboard.
- If you want to be a painter, sit in front of an easel.
- If you want to be an entrepreneur, start a business.

A good example is if one wants to be a writer, but they spend more time researching topics or other writers instead of sitting down and typing or putting pen to paper. If you want to be a good guitar player, of course, it is good to take note of the great guitar players. But to be a good guitar player yourself, you must actually play!

There is an order to your goal.

1. First, you learn the parts of the guitar.
2. Next, you learn how to properly tune your guitar.
3. Then, you would learn your scales and chords.
4. Before long, you will be learning to play actual songs.
5. The more that you practice, the better you will be.

What action can I take today to move forward in reaching my goal?

Start with some baby steps to snowball from there.

Date: _____

Goal:

_____

_____

_____

How will I achieve this goal:

_____

_____

_____

Goal:

_____

_____

_____

How will I achieve this goal:

_____

_____

_____

Goal:

_____

_____

_____

How will I achieve this goal:

_____

_____

_____

Goal:

_____

_____

_____

How will I achieve this goal:

_____

_____

_____

Concentrate on your Goals

Concentrate on your goals. You must keep focus by staying in the moment. Don't let yourself get distracted.

List your distractions (*TV, Youtube, video games, Facebook, etc.*):

Flip the Negative Thinking

If negativity has been getting in your way, you must flip your **thinking**. Instead of focusing on what you do not want in your life, turn your thoughts to what you do want. Another way to flip your thinking is to **think backwards**. If you know what your destination is, take the steps backwards to see how you get there.

For instance, if your goal is to be on Saturday Night Live, you will want to look at other people that have gotten to that point and see what steps they took to get there. They all have agents. Maybe before SNL, they were in improvisational comedy, which most were. From there, you would research which improv schools they came from. Then, you will realize that before they began performing improv, they had taken classes at that improv school. A diagram of this path may look something like this:

Improv School > Become a Cast Member of School > Get an Agent > SNL

What path do I need to take to get to where I want to go?

Step 1: _____

Step 2: _____

Step 3: _____

Step 4: _____

Step 5: _____

Use Your Imagination

Your **imagination** is a great tool. Visualize yourself doing what you want. Envision that you have already completed your goal and are successful. Use your internal control. Harness your brain's power with meditation.

What is success to me? What does it look like?

Set small, Obtainable goals

Set small, **obtainable** goals. Instead of focusing on how far away our goal may seem, taking baby steps to get there.

1) _____

2) _____

3) _____

4) _____

5) _____

6) _____

7) _____

8) _____

9) _____

10) _____

Determine Your Needs

We all have needs. They may be basic physiological needs like food, water, and shelter. They may be much more complex like realizing your purpose in life. The chart below shows Maslow's hierarchy of needs, which is a five-tier model of human needs. It is one of the best-known theories of human motivation. The higher needs come into focus once the lower level needs have been met. You will not be worried about recognition if you are starving.

Take a moment to think about your needs. Which ones are being met and which ones are lacking?

> *The story of the human race is the story of men and women selling themselves short. ~ Abraham Maslow*

What are my most urgent needs?

_____

_____

_____

_____

What do I need in order to reach my goal? (more money, more time, a degree, etc.)

_____

_____

_____

_____

_____

6 SMART GOAL SETTING

Set a few specific, measurable, achievable, realistic, and timely goals.

Specific: What do I want to do? How am I going to do it? Why?

Measurable: How will I know that I have achieved my goal? What is the date I want it done by? If I want to make more money, how much exactly do I want?

Attainable: Can this be done? Do I have the time, skills, energy, and money to do this?

Realistic: Can I really do this? Are these goals in line with my vision of success?

Timely: When do I want my goal completed by?

Think about my goal. Define it by the SMART goal setting method. How does it meet each category?

Specific	
Measurable	

Attainable	
Realistic	
Timely	

Write a mission statement

When you start a business, one of the first things that you do is to create a mission statement. It identifies what your organization does and gives the organization structure. It is the Who, What, When, Where, Why, and How of your organization. A personal mission statement is similar in that it identifies your core values and beliefs. It articulates what you are all about. It paints a picture of what success looks like to you.

To write your own personal mission statement, you must answer these questions:

- **WHO?** Who is your best you? Who are you creating this goal for? Who is your customer or audience?

_____

_____

_____

- **WHAT?** What is important to you? What do you want to do? What do you want to leave as your legacy? What are your skills, values, passions, or dreams?

_____
_____
_____

- **WHEN?** Do you have a timeframe you are working within? Where do you see yourself in one, five, or ten years?

_____
_____
_____

- **WHERE?** Where will this take place? Where do you want to go?

_____
_____
_____

- **WHY?** What is the purpose of your plan?

_____
_____

It does not have to be long. Just a line or two should sum up what you are in a clear and concise manner. An example would be: *"To inspire change and to positively impact the lives of everyone that I meet."* Oprah Winfrey's personal mission statement looks like this: *"To be a teacher. And to be known for inspiring my students to be more than they thought they could be."*

My mission statement:

_____

_____

_____

_____

_____

_____

Set intentions

What is my intention? Here are some examples:

- Find balance
- Open the mind and heart
- Peace
- Embrace change
- Love and to love unconditionally
- Connect with others
- To manifest happiness
- To lead by example

- Make someone smile each day

What are my intentions?

_____

_____

_____

Increase your Energy

Is the reason for your lack of motivation due to a lack of energy? What am I doing to increase my energy level?

- Meditation
- Exercise
- Eating healthy
- Taking a multi-vitamin
- Getting enough sleep

What changes can I make in my daily routine to increase my energy level?

_____

_____

_____

Values

What are my values?

In order to find your happiness, you have to assess what your values are.

What is really important to you?

Here is an example of common values. Select your top five values.

- Achievement
- Adventure
- Art
- Autonomy
- Awareness
- Balance
- Belonging
- Cleanliness
- Community
- Compassion
- Creativity
- Determination
- Empathy
- Fairness
- Friendships
- Fun
- Gratitude
- Growth
- Happiness
- Honesty
- Humor
- Independence
- Joy
- Others:

- Kindness
- Knowledge
- Love
- Loyalty
- Meaningfulness
- Openness
- Optimism
- Passion
- Patience
- Peace
- Persistence
- Recognition
- Respect
- Responsibility
- Security
- Solitude
- Spirituality
- Stability
- Success
- Trustworthiness
- Understanding
- Wealth
- Wisdom

Positive Affirmations

Positive affirmations are the pep talks that we give ourselves. If you remember the character Stuart Smalley from Saturday Night Live, Al Franken's character used daily affirmations to boost his self-esteem. His most popular affirmation was: "I'm good enough, I'm smart enough, and doggone it, people like me!"

Think about what you would like to change. Make sure that the affirmation that you choose is realistic. Saying "I'm going to double my income next week" may not be achievable. Make sure that they are positive and in the present tense. No "I'm going to", but rather "I am". Make sure there is emotion invested in your affirmation to give it strength. You need to believe it. "I AM capable."

Here are some examples of positive affirmations:

- I can do this.
- I am creative.
- I am successful.
- My peers respect me and value my opinion.
- I am grateful for my home and job.
- I am happy and excited.
- I exude positivity and enthusiasm.
- I am a kind person and deserve love.
- I am a beautiful person.
- I love myself unconditionally.
- I am fearless, strong, and passionate.
- I am calm and peaceful.
- I am aware of my full potential.
- There is no obstacle that I cannot overcome.
- Life is beautiful and amazing.
- I only attract positivity into my life.
- I am a better me today than I was yesterday.
- I am content. I am good enough.
- There is no limitation on what I can achieve.
- I am creating the path to my dreams.

Write down 3 positive affirmations and say them into the mirror each day for a week.

Affirmation #1
Affirmation #2
Affirmation #3

Write them down and put these affirmations in a place where you will see them often. Put the affirmations on post-it notes on your bathroom mirror or refrigerator. Use a cork board or dry erase board to display your affirmations. Repetition is the key.

Visualization Board

If you say it, you become it. Also, if you see it, you can be it. With visualization, you want to anticipate a positive outcome. You are seeing your goal as if it is already completed.

Take five to ten minutes each day to focus on your visualizations. Create a vision board. A vision board is a tool that you can use to put your goals into focus. They allow you to clarify what you want by giving it a tangible image that you can concentrate on. You can use a cork board or just copy images to a piece of paper or poster board to make your collage. I make my vision boards in a Word document on my computer with clips of various pictures and words.

What do I want to put on my vision board? Make a list of images, words, or anything that you want to put into your board. It could be your dream house or car, people you admire, images that involve the career that you want, or anything. Start by picking 5 things:

Item #1
Item #2
Item #3
Item #4
Item #5

7 EXERCISES

Meditation Exercise #1:

Take 10 minutes each day to sit in mindful meditation. We spend so much time either dwelling on the past or worrying about the future that we do not spend enough time in the moment. For 10 minutes each day, quietly sit, focus on your breathing, and just be present. Notice how your body feels. Notice all of the sounds, sights, and smells around you. Don't think about what you need to do today. Your grocery list can wait until later. Just be.

Meditation Exercise #2: Smile Meditation

Much like the first exercise, sit quietly for 10 minutes, focusing on your breathing, while continuously smiling. It does not have to be a huge grin, but a nice, relaxed smile. You will be amazed at how the act of smiling changes how you feel. If you have a scowl on your face, you are going to feel more grumpy and irritable. With a smile, you feel more at ease, peaceful, and dare I say, happy!

Gratitude Exercise #1:

Each day, write down 3 things that you are grateful for. These can things that happened or things you have. Even if you are having a bad day, you can think of at least 3 things for which you are grateful. Include why you are grateful for these things. Ex: I am grateful for: my bed because it is so soft, my dogs for their companionship and unconditional love, and being able to sleep in today to catch up on my lack of sleep and now I have more energy.

Repeat this each day for a week. Use the blank boxes below. Once you get into the habit, you will see the benefits of practicing gratitude. Start your own gratitude journal that you write in every day. You can get a notebook for 50 cents.

Day 1: Date
Gratitude 1
Gratitude 2
Gratitude 3

Day 2: Date
Gratitude 1
Gratitude 2
Gratitude 3

Day 3: Date
Gratitude 1
Gratitude 2
Gratitude 3

Day 4: Date
Gratitude 1
Gratitude 2
Gratitude 3

Day 5: Date
Gratitude 1
Gratitude 2
Gratitude 3

Day 6: Date
Gratitude 1
Gratitude 2
Gratitude 3

Day 7: Date
Gratitude 1
Gratitude 2
Gratitude 3

Gratitude Exercise #2:

Who are you grateful for? Think of 3 people that have had a positive influence on you. This could be a parent, child, teacher, boss, friend, or anyone who has had an impact on your life. This could be big or even as small as someone opened the door for you.

Who are you grateful for and why?

Person 1
Person 2
Person 3

Now pick one of these people and write to them to tell them how grateful you are to them. This could be an email, text, or hand-written letter. Take some time and be thoughtful in your words. Let them know how they have impacted you. How did they help you? Did they make you the person that you are today? If you'd rather meet them face-to-face to tell them, even better! Nothing beats the personal touch.

How did it make you feel? What was their reaction?

Random Acts of Kindness Exercise:

Do a good deed for the day. Go out of your way to make someone else's day a little bit better. Open the door for someone. Give someone a smile, hug, or compliment. Do at least one each day for a week.

Here is a list of some examples:

1) Compliment someone, even a stranger.
2) Volunteer at a homeless shelter.
3) Volunteer at an animal shelter.
4) Donate extra dog or cat food to an animal shelter.
5) Do a marathon for a good cause.
6) Pick up litter.
7) Let someone go in front of you in line.
8) Donate blood.
9) Pay for someone's meal at a restaurant.
10) Donate your old clothes to charity.
11) Hold the elevator for someone.
12) Do yard work for your neighbor.
13) Pay for someone else's coffee.
14) Spread some positivity online.
15) Snap a photo for a couple trying to take a selfie.
16) Perform at a retirement home.
17) Leave a generous tip for a server.
18) Mentor a child.
19) Send coloring books to a children's hospital.
20) Tutor a student.
21) Recycle.
22) Post inspirational post-it notes around the office.
23) Leave quarters at the laundromat or carwash.
24) Hold the door open for someone.
25) Make someone laugh.
26) Really listen to someone.
27) Let one car merge in front of you in traffic.
28) Have a conversation with a stranger.

29) Read to a child.
30) Visit someone who may be lonely.
31) Did you get good service today? Let the manager know.
32) Smile and say hello to a stranger.
33) Send an email to someone showing them your gratitude.
34) Give recognition to a co-worker. Let them know that they are doing a good job.
35) Return shopping carts at the grocery store to make less work for the employees.
36) While you're out, compliment a parent on how well-behaved their child is.
37) Pay the toll for the person behind you.
38) Learn the names of people you see daily (bank teller, security guard, etc.).
39) Keep an extra umbrella at work, so you can lend it out when it rains.
40) Put your phone away while in the company of others.

Day 1: Date
What did you do? Who was it for?

Day 2: Date
What did you do? Who was it for?

Day 3: Date
What did you do? Who was it for?

Day 4: Date
What did you do? Who was it for?

Day 5: Date
What did you do? Who was it for?

Day 6: Date
What did you do? Who was it for?

Day 7: Date
What did you do? Who was it for?

Try to incorporate doing "good deeds for the day" every day!

8 FIND BALANCE IN MY LIFE

In order to have happiness, you have to have a balanced life. One of the main philosophies of Taoism is to live in harmony and balance. Look at all of the areas of your life. See what needs some balance. You cannot have balance if the different areas of your life are not receiving equal attention from you. Your financials will struggle if you are spending most of your time and money on recreation. If you spend most of your focus on work, your family life will suffer. In the words of Jack from *The Shining*, "All work and no play makes Jack a dull boy."

In the following chart, make goals of what you want to achieve this year in each area of your life.

My Goals Areas:	What I want to achieve this year:
Health/Fitness	
Career/Work	
Family/Friends	
Relationship/Romance	
Personal Growth & Development	
Fun/Recreation	
Financial	
Spiritual	

Now that you have completed this workbook, you should have a better idea of what you want out of life and how to achieve it. Hopefully, you have started to incorporate new techniques into your life to reduce your stress and increase your happiness. Happiness is not external; it all comes from within. Thank you for starting this journey into a new phase in your life. Remember, a one thousand mile journey begins with one step.

"The way to get started is to quit talking and begin doing." ~ Walt Disney

Time is the most precious commodity that we have. Unlike money, it is finite in supply and cannot be replenished. Once it is gone, it is gone forever. This is why we must make the most of the time that we have. The great thing about time is that it is unbiased. It does not care what your age, race, sex, income, or religion is. You have the same as anyone else regardless. Whether you are rich or poor, black or white, male or female, your time is the same. It is not about how much time you have, but rather what you do with it.

Are you spending your time wisely or frittering it away? If you found that you only had one year left to live, how would you plan on spending it? Most of us are not given the luxury of knowing how much time we have. Therefore, to effectively utilize it, we may want to spend it as if we only have a short time left to get the most out of it. We want to maximize our productivity. If you are given a month to complete a project, there are many of us that fall into the procrastination trap and put it off until the last minute. How many of us actually take advantage of the extra time and put it to good use? It is not enough to set your goals, but you have to get serious about avoiding distractions.

Most of us claim that we do not have enough time. We spend one-third of our time in bed. Most of us spend twenty-five percent of our time at work. Somehow, we have to balance the rest of the time that we have getting chores finished, socializing, spending it with our family, and somewhere in there, find a few minutes to set aside and commit to pursuing our goals. Balance is the key. Without balance, we become stressed and lose sight of our happiness. It is crucial to balance all of the aspects of our lives: work, family, friends, goals, etc. It is quite a juggling act, but it is necessary to live a fulfilling life.

It is easy to use the excuse that we just simply do not have enough time. That is a fallacy. We have the same twenty-four hours a day that Gandhi, Mother Teresa, and Thomas Edison had. The difference between us and them is that they knew how to properly prioritize. Prioritize your time by deciding what items are important or crucial.

To properly utilize your time, you must identify your time-wasters and learn how to overcome them. These are the activities that squander our time and are not productive. This could include watching TV or surfing the internet. Make a journal to assess how you spend your time for a week. Write down every activity and how long you spend doing it. You may be surprised how much time you do squander. Was the time spent on certain activities important or crucial? If not, you may want to re-evaluate your choices.

Set Limits
Learn how to set limits. Always be punctual. You don't want to waste someone's time by being late. Make sure that meetings begin and end on time. Setting a structure can help to make the meeting more timely and efficient. Think about what you want to get out of the meeting before it begins. If you are the one organizing the meeting, ask yourself if the meeting is even necessary. Meetings can eat up a lot of time, so if you are having a meeting for the sake of having a meeting, rethink how that time could be better spent.

Get out of the habit of constantly checking your email throughout the day. They can be a distraction. If we spend our time constantly checking and answering emails, we will not get anything else done. Choose a time of day, maybe first thing in the morning, to check and answer emails. Set a time limit for doing so. If you have a lot of emails, set aside one hour out of your day for that task. Set an alarm on your phone to let you know when you have hit the one hour mark and stick to that limit. Start with answering the most recent emails first. If you are backlogged, your first inclination will be to answer the oldest emails, but what happens is new emails keep popping up, and some are probably related to one of the older ones. If you attack the newest ones first, you will be surprised how quickly you will knock those emails out.

Turn off all electronics before bed. Looking at your phone or tablet as you are trying to get ready for bed is damaging. The blue light that electronics emit is counterproductive to your sleep. It halts your body's production of melatonin. If you are on your smartphone looking at Facebook and have trouble falling asleep, now you know part of the reason why.

When you are around other people, make a habit of putting your electronics away. If you are constantly checking your phone at the dinner table, you are not being in the moment with the real people that are right there with you. It is not only a distraction, but it is downright rude.

Clutter can be the enemy. It can be a huge distraction. Some of us use our disorganization as a reason to put off our goals. *"I will work on my goal once I get my house clean."* Then, do it! Create three piles: Keep, Give Away, and Throw Away. If you have not used it in six months and you don't see yourself using it in six more months, get rid of it. If you think it could be of use to someone else, give it away. There are tons of shelters and thrift stores that would welcome your donation. They may also be tax deductible. If it is broken, worn out, or torn, recycle or toss it. If you haven't patched up that hole by now, you aren't going to. Quit creating more unnecessary tasks for yourself. *"But I spent a lot of money on these clothes. I'll try to sell them on eBay or consign them."* You have just given yourself another job to do! Do you really want to take the time to sell stuff, which is taking away time from your goal, to make a few bucks? The time that you will have to dedicate to doing that is more than likely not worth the small amount of money that you will make.

Why put off until tomorrow what you can do today! Procrastination is a major Achilles heel for most people. If your task falls under the important or urgent category, do it now. Once it is finished, you will feel so good about yourself and feel motivated to finish another task. Procrastination is only a way of putting off your success.

Take a break! I know you may be thinking, "I can't take a break. I have too much to do." Work for an hour, and then take a break for fifteen minutes, if possible. You need to regroup and refuel to avoid getting burned out and overwhelmed. Also, set time aside for meditation. Even ten minutes of meditation can be effective. It gives your brain a break, which may allow you to properly put things into perspective. It will help you manage time, because it will give you more balance.

Again as Jack Torrance says in *The Shining*, "All work and no play makes Jack a dull boy." You have to put time aside to stop and smell the roses. It is important to take the time to unwind from the stresses of the day.

Try out a few of these tips to de-stress:
- Take time to be alone and evaluate.
- Simplify your life. (eliminate what is not necessary)
- Deep, slow breathing.
- Do something each day that brings you joy.
- It's okay to say no.
- Exercise.
- Do the task "right now" – "tomorrow" never comes.
- Notice nature. – (also people, music, etc.)
- Do one thing, focused, at a time.
- Stay in the Present.
- Talk a walk in your neighborhood.
- Listen to your favorite music.
- Make a date night with your significant other.
- Be aware of the demands you put on yourself.
- Prioritize.
- Smile and laugh more.
- Stop and smell the roses.

Be Prepared
Preparation aids time management. If you are fumbling around trying to find materials, you are wasting time. Keep the items that you use on a regular basis close at hand, and put away the things that don't get as much use. Being properly prepared frees up that time. Have a system of organization helps in preparation. Having folders properly labeled will save you time when looking for a document. Make a folder for each product, that includes physical files, computer files, and email files. This will make it easier to locate what is needs and make your system more functional.

Trying to pick out what to wear can be a daunting task. We can end up unnecessarily wasting a lot of time over what should take a few seconds to do. To avoid this, pick out what you are going to wear the night before. You can do this right before you go to bed as you are doing your nightly routines to brushing your teeth and washing your face. Have them ready and laying on a chair or hanging on the door.

Spend the last ten minutes of your workday making a list of what you need to accomplish the following day. Have it sitting on your desk waiting for you. It is easier for me to think of what needs to be done the night before. If I wait until the next morning, I am busy waking up or can't remember what I said that I had wanted to do. Prepare by doing it the night before, and make sure that you look at it the next day. A list means nothing if you do not use it.

Prioritizing

Not all tasks carry the same weight. Some tasks have a higher priority than others. You have to look at your list of tasks and determine which ones are important, urgent, or neither. Mailing a package so that it arrives for a meeting in time is urgent. Making a yearly doctor's appointment is important. Watching a recording on your DVR that you have already seen twice is neither important nor urgent.

Sometimes you can free some time up for yourself by delegating tasks to other people. Do you have someone that you work with that you could trust to do this task? When I was a manager, I felt compelled to try to do everything myself. I was a bit of a perfectionist. I wasn't sure if someone else would do it as well as I wanted it done, so I took on a lot of unnecessary workload. I had to learn to delegate to others. After all, if I trained them, I should be able to trust them to do the job. It makes them a stronger and valued employee, gives them a sense of purpose, and lightens your load.

Make a schedule. Block off time to work on projects. This provides structure to keep one on track to meet deadlines. If the goal you want to set is important, you must make time for it. In your schedule, block off what task you want to work on to complete your goal. Get a daily planner that has hourly designations. This will also show you where you are spending your time.

9 RE-EVALUATE MY GOALS

This may seem repetitive, but that's the point. Getting you to repeat and re-evaluate your goals allows you to reinforce what is important to you and re-establish your commitment.

Goal #1

Write down your specific goal.

List the steps that you need to take to accomplish this goal.

1) _____

2) _____

3) _____

4) _____

5) _____

6) _____

7) _____

8) _____

9) _____

10) _____

What obstacles do you see getting in the way? And how will you deal with them?

1)

2)

3)

4)

5)

6)

7)

8)

9)

10)

List 3 strengths that you have that will help you stay on track.

1)

2)

3)

Who can help you?

1)

2)

3)

Goal #2

Write down your specific goal.

List the steps that you need to take to accomplish this goal.

1) _____

2) _____

3) _____

4) _____

5) _____

6) _____

7) _____

8) _____

9) _____

10) _____

What obstacles do you see getting in the way? And how will you deal with them?

1)

2)

3)

4)

5)

6)

7)

8)

9)

10)

List 3 strengths that you have that will help you stay on track.

1)

2)

3)

Who can help you?

1)

2)

3)

Goal #3

Write down your specific goal.

List the steps that you need to take to accomplish this goal.

1) _____

2) _____

3) _____

4) _____

5) _____

6) _____

7) _____

8) _____

9) _____

10) _____

What obstacles do you see getting in the way? And how will you deal with them?

1)

2)

3)

4)

5)

6)

7)

8)

9)

10)

List 3 strengths that you have that will help you stay on track.

1)

2)

3)

Who can help you?

1)

2)

3)

10 USING THE 13 TECHNIQUES

1. Diet
2. Exercise
3. Yoga
4. Meditation
5. Tai Chi
6. Reiki
7. Laughter
8. Aromatherapy
9. Herbalism
10. Journaling
11. Unplugging from Technology
12. Color Therapy
13. Music

In the *The Heart of Happiness*, the book went into detail on these 13 techniques for stress management. Some may seem redundant or obvious, but how many of them are you actively doing? Some may put Yoga and Tai Chi under the category of exercise, and they are, but they are so much more. Both practices get into mental and even spiritual level in addition to the physical level.

Try one or all of these techniques and make them habitual. All are beneficial to your health and many can be used complementary to your current medical treatments and therapies. But, of course, these should not be used in lieu of professional medical advice and supervision. And always consult with your physician before you start a new diet plan or exercise program.

Diet

Whole, fresh, and unprocessed foods give you energy and strength. When your diet consists of nutritious and sustaining foods, you are on your way to healthy and happy living. Eating organic is healthier because it contains fewer or no pesticides, preservatives, antibiotics, or growth hormones. It is like putting the higher octane gas into your tank.

Also, portion size is important. You don't want to "feel full" when you eat. You want to feel "satisfied". What that means is you don't want to eat so much that you feel miserable and think "I wish I wouldn't have eaten that last bite." You want to have the sensation of wanting more, but not necessarily feeling hungry. This allows your body room to work. If you overeat, your body becomes tired and needs to rest to digest. That slows down your metabolism, and hence, you gain weight. When you finish eating, you should not feel like you need a nap. Also, do not eat at least three hours before you go to bed for this same reason.

Remember, carbs are not the enemy. Lack of exercise and overeating are!

- **Incorporate more fruits and vegetables into your diet.** You can do this in a number of ways.
    - Buy a spiralizer and turn a zucchini into noodles to replace pasta.
    - Make sure you dinner plate is half green. Include salads, broccoli, spinach, kale, brussel sprouts, or green beans into your diet. You would be surprised at all of the great recipes that are available for brussel sprouts. And don't overload you salad with dressing.
    - Eat a baked potato, but cut back a little on the butter, cheese, and sour cream.

- **Reduce your consumption of meat.** Limit your intake of red meat to only a couple of times a week at most. Try eating more poultry and fish.
- **Eliminate the sweets and processed foods.** Limit sodas, pastries, candy, anything that comes in a box, and fast food.

What will you do to improve your diet?

_____

_____

_____

_____

_____

_____

Exercise

The American Heart Association suggests that, for overall cardiovascular health, we get at least 150 minutes of moderately-intensive aerobic activity at least five days per week.

Should you run out and get a gym membership this January? Not if you aren't going to use it. A key to sticking with an exercise regime is to pick activities that you actually enjoy. It won't feel like work if you like doing it. Some people enjoy hiking. Maybe you could take a class. Try tap dancing, karate, kickboxing, CrossFit, or Pilates. There are countless classes to choose from. They will help keep you active as well as give you the social interaction that you may need. Another way of keeping fit and social is to join a team. Do a search for teams in your area to join. There are bowling leagues, kickball teams, softball, flag football, or even cornhole (yes, that's a thing!). Variety in activity will keep you interested.

Find ways of getting more active. Americans are more sedentary than any other time in history. Find an activity that you can enjoy and stick with. Make it a habit.

- Walking
- Running
- Going to the gym
- Forest bathing
- Bowling
- Adult team sports (kickball, soccer, softball, dodgeball, etc.)
- Basketball
- Frisbee
- Cycling
- Swimming
- Kickboxing
- Aerobics class
- Pilates
- Yoga
- Tai Chi

What forms of exercise are you going to incorporate in your weekly life?

_____

_____

_____

_____

How many times a week will you participate in these activities?

_____

_____

_____

_____

Yoga

Unfortunately, yoga is not considered aerobic activity. However, it is thought that yoga can be used to improve heart health and reduce stress levels, especially as a preventative measure or after facing a cardiac event. Yoga has a plethora of benefits for those that suffer from heart disease. Yoga has been found to lower blood pressure, lower cholesterol, lower heart rate, reduce blood sugar levels, improve respiratory function, increase lung capacity, boost circulation and the immune system, reduces stress, anxiety, and depression, eliminates insomnia, and increase muscle tone and flexibility. It basically improves your overall health.

What is wonderful about yoga is that anyone can do it, regardless of physical ability or condition, age, or weight. It is also great for people who may have been out of an exercise routine for some time.

There should be a plethora of classes available in your area. Find some videos on Youtube, a DVD, or a book on yoga and begin practicing at home.

Commit to doing at least 20-minutes of yoga every day.

Meditation

Meditation is a practice of training your mind. Just as you can train your body through physical exercises, you can train your mind with meditation. What you are trying to do is "empty" your mind. You may think, *"Oh, sitting and thinking about nothing? That's easy."* It's not as easy as you think.

What is the point? The point is to make your mind calm, focused, and peaceful. The more calm and peaceful your mind is, the happier you will be. The more focused you become, the more productive you will be. Once you are more peaceful, you become more appreciative, compassionate, and kind. Like with breathing exercises, meditation will help you relax, relieve stress, energize yourself, along with other numerous other physical and psychological benefits. Meditation will help change your mind.

Begin a meditation practice. You can start small and build from there. Begin by sitting for 10 minutes and concentrate on your breathing. If you find closing your eyes difficult, try staring at an object like a flower or candle.

Meditation can be as simple as sitting with your spine straight or lying down in a comfortable position, closing your eyes, breathing naturally, and focusing your attention on your breath. You can start by just trying to do this for five minutes. See how you do.

When do you plan on doing your meditation practice? Mornings? Evenings?

_____

_____

_____

Tai Chi

These are ancient Chinese practices that combine slow, deliberate movements, meditation, and breathing exercises. Tai Chi and Qi Gong are forms of martial arts that can help your circulation, balance, and alignment. Chi or Qi (both pronounced "chee") literally means "energy" or "life force". They are low-impact moving meditations that involve standing and balancing. They can be done at any physical level and at any age. They are excellent physical activities for beginners as well as people with health conditions. Anyone can benefit from it. The intensity is low, so the impact on your joints and muscles is minimal. You will flow from position to position and do so in beautiful movements. Tai Chi and Qi Gong can be done indoors and outdoors. Comfortable shoes and loose clothes are a must. Otherwise, there is nothing else you need to do it.

Tai Chi classes may be a bit more difficult to find than yoga classes. If you have trouble finding classes, there are videos available on Youtube or Amazon Prime.

Reiki

Reiki is a Japanese spiritual healing art that comes from the word Rei, meaning "Universal Life" and Ki, meaning "Energy". It was developed in 1922 by Japanese Buddhist Mikao Usui, but it is not affiliated with any religion. This life energy flows through all living things. Reiki is a technique of reducing stress and increasing relaxation. A Reiki Practitioner will basically be "laying on hands", in which the practitioner places their hands lightly on or over the person's body.

See if you can find a Reiki practitioner in your area and sign up for a treatment. They are usually very affordable and powerfully affective.

Laughter

The benefits of laughter to the human body are nearly immeasurable. There are quite complex and sophisticated physiological reactions that happen when we laugh. Our bodies respond to these reactions in several ways. Firstly, there is a decrease in stress hormones, such as cortisol and adrenaline, as well as an increase in beta-endorphins (which lower feelings of depression), when we laugh. Your body responds to laughter even if it is self-induced, or forced, laughter. Laughter also prompts the body to produce more T-cells, which boost our immune systems. People who laugh more tend to live longer and tend to be healthier overall.

Humor is a great functioning tool to use against stress. It can be a self-defense mechanism. There is a strong link between laughter and mental health. Start by simply **smiling**. Smiling will make you physically feel better. According to Scientific American, making an emotional face influences your feelings.

This one is easy. Watch a comedy or a video of your favorite comedian. Watch things that really make you belly laugh.

Make a list of your favorite funny movies. Make it a point to watch them.

1)

2)

3)

4)

5)

6)

7)

8)

9)

10)

Aromatherapy

Aromatherapy and the use of essential oils can reduce stress as well as aid in improving and preventing heart disease. A study published in the European Journal of Preventative Cardiology found that aromatherapy is beneficial in reducing stress.

Smell is a powerful tool toward stress management. Here are some ways of incorporating scent into your daily life.

- Essential oils (You can diffuse them or apply them topically. Make sure you purchase them from a reputable company. Don't just trust what the bottle says.)
- Treat yourself to a facial scrub or body and massage oils containing essential oils.
- Incense
- Fresh cut flowers
- Plant flowers

Herbalism

Evidence of plants being used medicinally dates back to the Paleolithic era. In some areas of the world, herbs are most people's main source of medicine. They not only are used to aid in ailments, but also used supplements as a preventative measure. Herbal medicine can be administered in a number of ways, including: teas, infusions, decoctions, tinctures, bolus, douche, enema, inhalation, liniments, oils, poultices, salves, and syrups.

Herbs are used by us daily in cooking, and they have a wonderful affect on our bodies.

- Make sure that your cupboard is full of a variety of herbs and spices to be used in your food. (Also, cooking can be quite relaxing.)
- Grow herbs in your garden.
- Use fresh herbs in your cooking, salads, and beverages.
- Enjoy an herbal tea.

Journaling

Another way to deal with stress is by journaling. In addition to helping you reduce stress, it can also sharpen your memory, boost your mood, and strengthen your emotional functions. Some studies even suggest that journaling can strengthen and improve the immune system. It enhances your communications skills, both verbally and written, as well as your reading skills. It can help you set and meet goals. Journaling can also improve your quality of life.

You can write about your day, your thoughts, or your feelings. Here are some ways to journal.

- Documenting your daily life
- Writing about gratitude
- Journaling about your emotions from day to day to see if there are patterns
- Journal about your progress in pursuing your goals

Unplugging from Technology

With social media being so predominant in today's society, we are constantly on our phones, tablets, and laptops, scrolling through our feeds. If we aren't doing that, we are playing video games and watching TV. Technology has opened us up to more information than no other generation before us. But all of this freedom has made us quite closed off. We have created our own little prisons via Facebook and Twitter. We spend countless hours checking our phones and updating our statuses. This is time that could have been better spent working on projects, focusing on our goals, reading a book, or even communicating with real people!

Unplugging may prove to be the most difficult. But if you succeed, you find that so much more time will be available to you. Not counting using social media for your business, how much time do you spend on the various platforms, i.e. Facebook, Youtube, Twitter, etc?

Plan more social activities to replace social media. Make plans with friends for dinner or to see a movie.

1)

2)

3)

4)

Color Therapy

If you are stressed, green and blue are two great colors to have around. Both have a relaxing and calming effect. Paint a wall one of these colors. According to a

Travelodge survey, those who have blue bedrooms sleep an average of seven hours and fifty-two minutes each night. Those whose bedrooms were red had the worst sleep. So if you have trouble sleeping, paint the walls blue or throw on a blue comforter. Invest in some blue or green pillows. Add some green plants into your home. Plants will add oxygen into your environment, and the color is soothing.

Green and blue are relaxing colors. Yellow and orange are happier colors.
- Wear a green shirt
- Buy some blue pillows
- Paint your bedroom blue
- Add more plants to your living room
- Paint your kitchen yellow
- Use blue plates

How can you incorporate color into your life?

_____

_____

_____

_____

Music

It is proven that music improves the health and function of our brains. By listening to and playing music, we become more intelligent and happier regardless of our stage of life. Children who study music and the arts do better in Math and Science. Stanford University of Medicine investigated the power of music on the mind, and they found that when people listen to music, their attention spans can be increased.

Music has been studied for centuries as to its affect on the human condition. Set some time aside to really enjoy music.

- Listen to music on your commute.
- Enjoy some music during dinner instead of the TV.
- Listen to music while you are doing homework or chores.
- Let's start again. Now that you've completed the workbook, review what you have done and how your goals have changed.

Day 1	Date:
Activities	**Time Spent Daily**
Sleeping	
Getting ready for the day *(shower, breakfast, getting dressed, etc.)*	
Working	
Commute	
Leisure *(TV, games, reading, etc,)*	
Eating	
Exercise	
Social	
Chores *(laundry, cleaning, etc.)*	
Shopping	
School, learning	
Other	

Day 2	Date:
Activities	**Time Spent Daily**
Sleeping	
Getting ready for the day *(shower, breakfast, getting dressed, etc.)*	
Working	
Commute	
Leisure *(TV, games, reading, etc,)*	
Eating	

Exercise	
Social	
Chores *(laundry, cleaning, etc.)*	
Shopping	
School, learning	
Other	

Day 3	Date:
Activities	**Time Spent Daily**
Sleeping	
Getting ready for the day *(shower, breakfast, getting dressed, etc.)*	
Working	
Commute	
Leisure *(TV, games, reading, etc,)*	
Eating	
Exercise	
Social	
Chores *(laundry, cleaning, etc.)*	
Shopping	
School, learning	
Other	

Day 4	Date:
Activities	**Time Spent Daily**
Sleeping	
Getting ready for the day *(shower, breakfast, getting dressed, etc.)*	
Working	
Commute	
Leisure *(TV, games, reading, etc,)*	
Eating	
Exercise	
Social	
Chores *(laundry, cleaning, etc.)*	
Shopping	
School, learning	
Other	

Day 5	Date:
Activities	**Time Spent Daily**
Sleeping	
Getting ready for the day *(shower, breakfast, getting dressed, etc.)*	
Working	
Commute	
Leisure *(TV, games, reading, etc,)*	
Eating	
Exercise	
Social	
Chores *(laundry, cleaning, etc.)*	
Shopping	
School, learning	
Other	

Day 6	Date:
Activities	**Time Spent Daily**
Sleeping	
Getting ready for the day *(shower, breakfast, getting dressed, etc.)*	
Working	
Commute	
Leisure *(TV, games, reading, etc,)*	
Eating	
Exercise	
Social	
Chores *(laundry, cleaning, etc.)*	
Shopping	
School, learning	
Other	

Day 7	Date:
Activities	**Time Spent Daily**
Sleeping	
Getting ready for the day *(shower, breakfast, getting dressed, etc.)*	
Working	
Commute	
Leisure *(TV, games, reading, etc,)*	
Eating	
Exercise	
Social	
Chores *(laundry, cleaning, etc.)*	
Shopping	
School, learning	
Other	

Now re-evaluate your goals one more time. Define you WHO, WHAT, WHERE, WHEN, HOW, AND WHY!

What is it that you want?

_____

_____

_____

_____

Who is my customer/audience?

_____

_____

_____

_____

Where do you see this happening?

_____

_____

_____

_____

When do you want to do this?

_____

_____

_____

_____

How will you accomplish this goal?

_____

_____

_____

_____

And most importantly, why are you doing this? Why is this goal so important to you?

_____

_____

_____

_____

ABOUT THE AUTHOR

Christy may be a comedian, but this is a serious book. It's a very serious topic and one that we see affecting many of our comedians past and present. It is a perfect topic for a comedian to cover because, as a group, most comedians are affected by anxiety and depression. We use humor as a coping mechanism in dealing with stress in our search for happiness. We search and search for exterior elements to make us happy, but that won't happen, at least not for the long-run. True happiness comes from within.

Christy has been doing standup for over 15 years. She has been suffering from anxiety and depression for twice as long. It has taken her decades of trial and error to figure out what works for her to cope.

Christy makes the material relatable by using pop culture references to illustrate her points.

www.ingramcontent.com/pod-product-compliance
Lightning Source LLC
Chambersburg PA
CBHW080936170526
45158CB00008B/2305